PHILOSOPHY of the INNER LIGHT

MICHAEL MARSH

✧ Pendle Hill Pamphlet 209 ✧

About the Author / Michael Marsh was born in New York City on February 2, 1918. He became "glancingly acquainted with Quakerism," as he puts it, at Swarthmore College, at an AFSC work camp (where he met his wife, Caryl), and in civilian public service during World War II. Riper acquaintance led to his joining the Friends Meeting of Washington in 1952, but only in recent years has he become a seeker. Professionally he has been an economic researcher, a foreign correspondent, and a labor lobbyist, and is currently an associate editor of the newspaper *Labor*. In 1975 he was granted an M.A. degree in philosophy by Catholic University of America.

As for the present publication, let Michael speak for himself: "This pamphlet grew out of my own experience. That included a good bit of thinking as well as feeling. I hope the pathway I've found may prove useful to others who dwell, as I did, in an unhappy skepticism. The American intellectual establishment accepts material reality and social reality; it has a dogmatic disbelief in spiritual reality. This dogma of disbelief often intensifies human anguish. The way out, I think, lies neither in irrationalism nor despair but in using and understanding the inner light."

ISBN 0-87574-209-2
Library of Congress catalog card number 76-50674

Printed in the United States of America by
Sowers Printing Company, Lebanon, Pennsylvania

November 1976: 3,000

THIS IS THE STORY of a seeking and finally a finding. It began in Friends meetings for worship. It went on to the study of various great philosophers in the Western tradition. It came back, enriched, to meeting for worship. The goal of my search was meanings. What *is* the inner light—or, as George Fox and other early Quakers called it—the "light within"? What is "that of God in every one"? I wasn't asking here for definitions. Rather, I sought to know how the inner light operates, how it can be used, most of all what it signifies. I'd had enough of subjective interpretations, of sociological religion; what I needed to find was some objective truth. Is it true that the inward light is a seed of God in me? But what is God?

My goal was not to chase words but to uncover the value of my life: to discover what it means to be human. I found in myself a great thirst. In my middle years I became again an adolescent asker of questions. I began to explore and ultimately to find.

I'd like to convey to you some of these findings. But how fruitful they seem will depend on where you are. If your own inner experience is so rich that you feel no need to test it against other knowledge, then what I have to say may seem bare and useless. So, too, if Holy Scripture is your final authority. Those who discover some value in my account will be, I think, the doubters who seek, the unsatisfied humanists, the troubled skeptics, all those who view themselves in *reality* as momentary specks of protoplasm on an orbiting dot near one of a hundred billion stars, in one galaxy among a billion other galaxies in a meaningless universe. To you then who view *reality* in this drear way, who have only half-hopes, half-beliefs because reason and science seem to forbid you more, I address what follows.

HISTORY OF THE CONCEPT

My first discovery proved to me my own ignorance. For some reason I had considered George Fox to be the inventor of the inward light as an explanatory concept. I'd thought of this notion as a patented Quaker idea. Of course, I realized the Gospel of John spoke of Jesus Christ as "the true Light, which lighteth every man that cometh into the world." But this seemed to me a mystery statement, a bald assertion of faith. So too with those Oriental religions that told of unearthly lights. Fox, I thought, was the first to speak experientially of a light within that opens one's understanding and reveals one's way.

The facts, I found, are quite otherwise. Many philosophers and religious seers in the West, from Plato onwards, have written of the inner light as the foundation of our knowing, as a Godlike capacity in us, or even as a manifestation of God to us. Beginning with Plato, a very partial listing would include such leaders of Western thought as Philo Judaeus, St. John the Evangelist, the early Gnostics, Plotinus in the third century, St. Augustine in the fourth and fifth; in the Middle Ages, St. Bonaventure, St. Thomas Aquinas, Dante, Meister Eckhart; in the seventeenth century, the great mystic Jakob Boehme, and our own George Fox and, as well, the founders of modern philosophy: Descartes, Locke, Berkeley, Leibniz. One hears less of the inner light in the nineteenth and twentieth centuries as other terms and explanations push forward in philosophy. Even today, though, the existentialist Martin Heidegger writes of an inner "clearedness" in a sense very close to our use of inner light.

These discoveries buoyed me. When Quakers speak of a light within, we're not dealing with some esoteric idea of our own. We're dealing, rather, with a concept that has appealed to some of the greatest minds in the history of the planet. But what meaning did these minds give to the concept?

LIGHT AS A METAPHOR

First of all, several philosophers stated explicitly that the term "inner light" is a metaphor. We are comparing what happens within us, in our minds, with what happens outside us, in a world lit by physical light. As a metaphor, we speak of the light inside resembling the light outside. In what ways are they similar? For one thing, so far as our experience goes, both kinds of light function only part of the time. They function, in our experience, variably: sometimes bright, sometimes dim, sometimes leaving us in darkness. The greatest outward light, the sun, not only illumines but also warms, enabling organisms to grow: so too the inward light both illumines and enables the mind to grow. Outer light comes from various sources: the sun, the moon, fire, electricity. Inner light comes from—where? That question, so crucial to my search, I found very hard to answer; the answer I did reach I shall describe later on.

Most happily I discovered from the philosophers that neither the outer light nor the inner light need be visible in itself. Rather, the light *makes visible*. Sunlight is the medium that reveals to us objects in the world. We see the objects *by means of* the light. They are made visible to us. We usually don't see the light itself. Indeed on a cloudy day it may be impossible to find the sun at all; or in an indirectly lit room it may be impossible to discover the source of light. Instead physical light, as a medium, reveals to us the outer objects toward which we look with our eyes. Even so, the inner light as a medium reveals to us ideas or relationships—that is, mental realities—toward which we open our mind's eye.

To me it came as a revelation that I didn't have to see the inner light in order to use it and believe in it. At first—I was then in my thirties—I had sat in meetings for worship Sunday after Sunday, trying to open myself to the light within. Never once did I see anything like a light. This discouraged me so much that for some years I attended meeting only rarely. Finally, after learning from the philosophers that I need not *see* the light, I came back to meeting. I began to practice the presence of the light and found that I could use it.

Before exploring ways to use the light, let's note that some people do at times *see* an intense and extraordinary spiritual light; this they identify not as hallucinatory but as divine. So with Paul on the road to Damascus. So with Pascal who experienced for two hours one night "FIRE—God of Abraham, God of Isaac, God of Jacob, not of the philosophers and the learned." So with St. Augustine, who tells us:

> I entered into my inmost being . . . and by my soul's eye, such as it was, I saw above that same eye of my soul, above my mind, an unchangeable light. It was not this common light, plain to all flesh, nor a greater light, as it were, of the same kind, as though that light would shine many, many times more bright, and by its great power fill the whole universe. Not such was that light, but different, far different from all other lights. Nor was it above my mind, as oil is above water, or sky above earth. It was above my mind, because it made me, and I was beneath it, because I was made by it. He who knows the truth knows that light, and he who knows it knows eternity. Love knows it, O eternal truth, and true love, and beloved eternity! You are my God, and I sigh for you day and night! *(Confessions,* tr. John K. Ryan, Bk. 7, Ch. 10).

Those who experience such visions say they are left with a certainty of being in touch with God. But what are we, who have not seen, to make of their testimony? Visionary experience alone is no test of objective truth. There are, however, some ways of using the inner light that *don't* depend on visions.

SEEING INWARDLY

Human experience discloses at least four major perspectives in which a light of the mind seems to operate. These perspectives, though distinct, are inter-related. The perspectives are truth, love, moral rightness and beauty. Each of these provides us with a kind of meaning. Often we call this meaning an *insight,* that is, a seeing-in. We see-in to events, feelings, ideas or other experiences in a new way, using that capacity known as the inner light to reveal until-now-hidden relationships within a perspective. The insight into meaning may be positive or negative. I may see the newly grasped state of affairs as true or not-true, love or not-love, right or not-right, beautiful or not-beautiful. Also, as George Fox pointed out, each of us has a different measure of light available, whether from our differing endowments or differing skill in using the light. Thus the level of insight will vary. Another important point is that the process of revelation is not always so passive as when we sit quietly in Friends meeting or in private meditation; many insights may come while we are actively making, doing, or creating in the world. Let's consider how we use our capacities in each of the four perspectives.

PERSPECTIVE OF TRUTH

In *truth* the simplest and most immediate insights are the relations available in perception here and now: this button is above that one, these three apples are more than those two apples, and so on. These insights may seem so simple as to be scarce worth mention. This kind of knowledge, however, serves as the foundation of all we know about the world. As John Locke observed, it is "irresistible and, like bright sunshine, forces itself immediately to be perceived, as soon as ever the mind turns its view that way." A second kind of irresistible knowledge is less direct. These are the truths laid bare by logical or mathematical proofs or demonstrations, for example, that the three inner angles of a Euclidean triangle are equal to two right angles. We may find it hard at first to follow the chain of reasoning involved in such a demonstration. But once we *see* it, in a flash of insight, we are forever afterwards certain of it.

A third kind of truth that we see inwardly is explanations. Here there's substantial chance for error but we often do reach the truth. Thus I brought home a new lawn mower in a box and found I'd have to assemble it myself. Instead of following the instructions by rote I pondered and *saw* how the different parts must fit; then I easily put them together. Again, I came home the other day and found unexplained liquid on the living room floor, along with a couple of green leaves. In imagination I *saw* a vase of flowers toppled over, my wife discovering and removing it, but not yet having wiped up the water. So too with the explanations for all other events we have not directly experienced. To know their truth we must picture these events somehow with our mind's eye. At times the explanations even contradict our own experience. Thus no experience seems more evident than the sun's movement each day from east to west around the earth; but we now *see* the true explanation as earth-in-motion, for the Copernican insight explains the planetary motions as a whole more simply and harmoniously than our own direct experience does. As Leibniz observed, "It is only with the eyes of the understanding that we can place ourselves in a point of view which the eyes of the body do not and cannot occupy."

A twentieth century philosopher, W. E. Hocking, describes the process well: "The thinker's mind, bent on his inarticulate goal, as if in prayer, encounters blank nescience; and then one day comes a swift light, unpredictably transforming both the vista and the viewer; not as a gift from prearranged discernments, but through some intimate cooperation of thinker and objects, comes the viable idea striving for birth: 'Now I see!' " Without that capacity for inward vision neither science nor art could exist. Yet the inward vision alone does not suffice; it must prove itself in the outer world. Its truth must be tested.

PERSPECTIVE OF LOVE

A second perspective for inward vision is *love*. One can define love broadly as any attraction, any impulsion-toward. How cold that sounds! And love, we know, is the warmest of feelings. The first slight gasp of love and one's veins seem touched by fire. The other person takes on a new light. One's own eyes must shine so bright they'll betray what's within; one fears to frighten the other; one must keep the voice calm, the laughter amiable. A whole new world begins to build. . . . And apart from these man-woman or unisexual attractions we experience, as well, love for a parent, a child, a brother or sister, another relative, a friend new or old.

Any human love, I think, partakes of three levels of feeling, but in very different proportions. First, the love we experience grows out of animal appetite. We seek our own sensual pleasure. Some brief loves rise very little above this primal level. But no actual human that I've known or heard of ever divested his or her love of all further meaning. On the other hand, not even the highest upward displacement of love—such as Spinoza's intellectual love of God or the love in mystical union—can free itself utterly of the appetitive base, so long as the lover remains human.

At the second level we feel love as an attraction to, and appropriation of, objects. We seek to possess. We desire to take the love object, to extend our self by enveloping it, to make of the object our property. When directed toward other persons this kind of love poses obvious problems. Another person can never be truly my property. This kind of love may be displaced, however, onto different life goals: onto work-objects, play-objects, creative-objects, a variety of material possessions. Here the opportunities for achievement and satisfaction are greater than in possessive love toward another person. But a degree of detachment toward all possessions may serve us best.

The third level of love rises to empathy with the inwardness of the other person. It treats the other as subject, not as object. The other becomes not my possession but my other self. Here I develop the I-Thou relation. With mutual love, it's *we* who grow into the I-Thou relation. Here one enters the most enchanting and at times most frustrating of human experiences. Since the other's subjectivity is never perceptible by my outward senses, I must always seek it through my own inner light: interpreting, questioning, imagining. So long as I exist primarily on this level of loving (though pulled often below it, to appetitive and possessive love or to not-love), so long do I gain some access to my beloved's inner being, but never the full unity I yearn for.

All human loves, I suggested, participate to a degree in each of the three levels—sensual appetite, possessive desire for the love-object, and yearning to unite with the other's subjectivity. Some of us experience a fourth level, as well, in loving God. Whatever the objective reality of this love-relation with God, its subjective reality appears in two distinct ways. We may find ourselves in a holy, awesome, separate, transcendent presence, perhaps accompanied by visions or words, to which we reach out in humble love, often feeling God's love in return. Or we may experience an extraordinary mystical union with a presence undefined, all seeming empty and yet filled with unending love. As John Ruysbroek wrote:

> We follow the splendor of God on toward the source from which it flows, and there we feel that our spirits are stripped of all things and bathed beyond all thought of rising in the pure and infinite ocean of love. This *immersion in love* becomes the habit of our

being, and so takes place while we sleep and while we wake, whether we know it or whether we know it not. (Quoted by Rufus Jones, *Studies in Mystical Religion,* p. 311).

In either version God may also illumine us. We then experience the radiance of an unearthly loving light.

PERSPECTIVE OF RIGHTNESS

In the perspective of *rightness* we also find a kind of light at work. Every normal person develops internalized guides for conduct, going beyond self-serving standards. Such a guide invokes the moral "ought." I must do this, or refrain from doing that, not out of prudence but because I ought to, because it's right. Whence comes this moral guide? Sigmund Freud suggested the source is parental authority, which the young child internalizes into a "super-ego" composed of a conscience that forbids and an ego-ideal that urges forward. Other psychologists, most notably Jean Piaget and Lawrence Kohlberg, have uncovered progressive stages of moral development as the child grows through adolescence into adulthood. Kohlberg found successive stages of morality that he labelled pre-conventional, conventional and post-conventional. These stages appear in different cultures, but only a minority of people reach the post-conventional or highest stage.

Now conventional morality varies notoriously in different eras and different cultures. Yet certain maxims are very widespread. These include the Golden Rule and such other propositions, cited by St. Augustine, as "man ought to live justly; the worse ought to be subject to the better; like is to be compared with like; each man should be given his due." One also finds a wide admiration for those who rise above conventional morality in their own lives, aspiring to live by higher standards. Often, as Augustine observes, "even the unrighteous recognizes what is righteous . . . he discerns that he ought to have what he himself has not.'' Even the unrighteous can read ''in the book of that Light which is called Truth.'' Even so, the person who finally accepts the guide of rightness is said to ''see the light.''

More broadly, the inner light in its moral perspective amounts to a capacity within us to achieve that perspective. This capacity lies in us, waiting to be used, no matter what the moral maxims we actually have absorbed and seek to apply. However, human experience suggests that the light in its moral aspect is not inert. The more I can free myself from passion, desire, and interest, and open myself to the pure morality of the light, the higher it will pull me. Indeed it may pull me too high. The moral light is not all of me, and any one perspective, followed alone, will twist me out of shape.

PERSPECTIVE OF BEAUTY

In the perspective of *beauty* we view things with new eyes. We see them—or hear, touch, smell, taste them—not as instruments toward our goals but as valuable in themselves. The standard for judging whether a natural scene, a house, a car, an art object, a performance, a person, a situation, a relationship is beautiful is the breadth and depth of its harmony. Part of that harmony involves internal relations. Part involves fulfillment of function.* Part involves an expansible set of outer relations. This complexity of harmonic relations, and the variability of backgrounds and tastes that each one of us brings to it, account for the wide variations in judgments of beauty. Thus anyone's judgment of beauty, viewed from outside, seems largely subjective. Viewed from within me,

---

*If its function includes serving me, then love for it often warps my judgment of its beauty.

however, beauty seems wholly out there: the object *is* beautiful, producing a kind of silent music, a resonance of be-ing, which speaks not of itself alone but of greater things. And this evokes in me a unique happiness, usually quite serene, and sometimes deep.

The full experience of beauty may separate me from my self almost as much as does mystical love. Thus the art critic Bernard Berenson writes in his memoirs: "I have never enjoyed to the utmost a work of art of any kind, whether verbal, musical or visual, never enjoyed a landscape, without sinking my identity into that work of art, without becoming it, although . . . a miniscular observer is always there, watching, noting, appreciating, estimating, judging . . ." This "sinking my identity" is a capacity made available by a certain aspect of the light within, which serves as the phenomenological ground between subject and object.

Apart from enjoyment of beauty, many seek to make beauty. Here, as in the discovery of truth, the inner light serves the seeker as a creative field. At times the light appears as carrier of a revelation, a divination; at others it's the medium for shaping creative ideas. So Nietzsche, describing the composition of his poetic *Thus Spake Zarathustra:* "The notion of revelation describes the condition quite simply; by which I mean that something profoundly convulsive and disturbing suddenly becomes visible and audible with indescribable definiteness and exactness. One hears—one does not seek; one takes—one does not ask who gives: a thought flashes out like lightning, inevitably without hesitation—I have never had any choice about it."

Or Picasso: "How would you have a spectator live my picture as I have lived it? A picture comes to me from far off, who knows how far, I divined it, I saw it, I made it, and yet next day I myself don't see what I have done." Henry Moore is more explicit, recounting that the sculptor "gets the solid shape, as it were, inside his head—he thinks of it, whatever its size, as if he were holding it completely enclosed in the hollow of his head. He mentally visualizes a complex form *from all around itself:* he knows while he looks at one side what the other side is like; he identifies himself with its centre of gravity, its mass, its weight; he realizes its volume, as the space that the shape displaces in the air."

William Blake had his own inner eye: "I see everything I paint in this world but everybody does not see alike. To the eye of a miser a guinea is far more beautiful than the sun and a bag worn with the use of money has more beautiful proportions than a vine filled with grapes. . . . When the sun rises, do you not see a round disk of fire something like a gold piece? O no, no, I see an innumerable company of the Heavenly host crying, 'Holy, Holy, Holy, is the Lord God Almighty.' I do not question my bodily eye any more than I would question a window concerning sight. I look through it and not with it." So do artists use the light within them, conscious and unconscious.

Some philosophers have found in beauty the highest of values. Thus Alfred North Whitehead suggested that "the adventure of the universe starts with the dream (of youth) and reaps tragic Beauty . . . that the suffering attains its end in a Harmony of Harmonies." Whatever ranking one assigns to beauty, rightness, love, and truth, the fact is clear that each of these inter-related perspectives gives *meaning* to our lives. Each perspective offers us meaningful interpretations, drawing on our past experience but going beyond that experience. And a second fact seems equally clear: Each of these perspectives operates by means of a capacity that enlightens, and that we may therefore call an inner light.

USING THE INNER LIGHT

I began now to see how I might use the inner light to help with my own problems. I began to grasp why George Fox urged early Friends to "stand still in the light," to be "still and cool," to "wait in the Light for Power to remove the earthly part." Do not look, he advised, "at the temptations, confusions, corruptions, but at the light that discovers them, that makes them manifest; and with the same light you will feel over them, to receive power to stand against them." This was how I might use meeting for worship. I could use it to open myself to a perspective of the light on my own needs. And so I began to do, based on some advice from Quaker authors. This technique does not always work, but I found it working enough of the time to be of real value. Here's what I learned to do:

I bring to meeting a problem, perhaps with full awareness of it, perhaps only half-consciously. It may be a question of why someone has picked a quarrel with me. It may be whether to start a new project. It may be a personal weakness or emotion that I find upsetting. Or a money problem. Or a purely intellectual question. I bring this to meeting in the back of my mind, but I don't begin by thinking about it. I need to distance it, to lay it quietly in the light. But having carried it to meeting with me, it's already *in* the light, unbeknownst. I simply have to let it emerge in freedom, though this is not always easy.

What happens in meeting is that I first try to settle, taking a relaxed posture, absorbing the room and people, laying aside the trip there and the morning's earlier events. I begin to center down by focussing on the lighted overhang of the wall opposite me, on a window, or on any still object. Thoughts drift through me. I examine them and lay them aside. Thoughts now come more slowly. Then a wisp—a little edge of thought—or perhaps a swift flash—and if I'm alert to it, and open, I find that more emerges and what I've been given is a new view of the problem

I brought with me. Sometimes, too, a spoken message helps me. This can develop now much further, if I continue open. I may now get round my problem as Henry Moore gets round his imagined statue. Sometimes what emerges is a new insight only. More often this carries with it a call to act in a certain way.

I still find this approach very helpful. But it seems now less complete than it did when I began it, a couple of years ago. Then, I felt delighted with my discoveries. I was finally *using* Friends meeting, getting practical help. Meeting for worship added real value to one's life. Meeting for *worship?*

Clearly I wasn't worshipping. I was making use of my own mental powers, of that capacity that we call, as a metaphor, an inward light. I still didn't *see* any light at all. I saw no visions. I heard no voices. I neither quaked nor trembled. Every once in a while I would center down so far that I'd pass into emptiness for a moment or two. Was that the light itself, with no objects in it? If so, it seemed trivial. It appeared to me simply empty, a waiting void. Surely I'd need more evidence before identifying this emptiness as a seed of God in me, or the inner light as a manifestation of God. Now I found I was not at the end of my search but still in the midst of it. I must seek further. I must answer: What *is* the inner light, not as a metaphor but in reality?

NATURAL OR DIVINE?

On this question I discovered a deep division among philosophers and religious thinkers. Many speak of a natural light of reason. Often they conceive this as created anew in each one of us, growing in us as we mature. Some believe also that our natural light can tap eternal ideas and principles. At the other pole some hold the inner light is divine, a candle of God within each human being. And since God is viewed as creator, not creat*ed*, this light is uncreated, pure, and eternal. Here George Fox stands, and most mystics. Others espouse a middle position. Thus St. Thomas Aquinas claimed that our inner light is "a participated resemblance of the uncreated (divine) light."

This seemingly arid debate began to plague me. I wanted to drop it. Why not simply believe? Why not simply accept that I was using a divine light within—accept the word of Scripture, the word of Fox, the word of so many other Quakers and mystics? But ignorant, unjustified belief would plunge a dagger into my innermost being. How many millions of people have been swayed by unjustified beliefs, even noble beliefs, into foolish or wicked acts. How many crimes have been committed in the name of religion; how many bloody wars, tortures, burnings at the stake in the name of faith! No, I could not *simply* believe. And yet, perpetual doubt seemed equally stupid. For I must live my life whether I doubt or believe, and the life inspired by doubt will inevitably stand for something. What it stands for will be either unconscious belief (from childhood) or meaningless nihilism. I can't escape choosing. Let me choose then with clear and open mind.

I came upon John Locke's middle position and a good bit of it sounded sensible. "The strength of our persuasions," Locke suggested, "is no evidence at all of their own rectitude: crooked things may be as stiff and inflexible as straight." The person who "will not give himself up to all the extravagances of delusion and error must bring this guide of his light within to the trial" of reason. When God "illuminates the mind with supernatural light," Locke continued, "he does not extinguish that which is natural. . . . *Reason must be our last judge and guide in everything." (Essay,* Bk. IV, Ch. XIX, Secs. 11, 14. Locke's italics.) This seemed to fit with the advice of the Quaker philosopher Rufus Jones. A sound spiritual religion, Jones held, should "supplement its more or less capricious and subjective, and always fragmentary, mystical insights with the steady and unwavering testimony of Reason, and no less with the immense objective illumination of History." *(Quakerism: A Spiritual Movement,* p. 96).

TESTS FOR TRUE BELIEF

So what tests does reason suggest for the truth of any belief? Five such tests are widely used. None is certain; not even all together can they yield utter certainty. But the more of them that are satisfied, the more justified one becomes in holding to the belief. Would these tests not apply also in justifying a belief that the light within me is divine? Here are the five tests:

1. *Ease of mind or absence of doubt.* This applies especially to my own experiences. Generally I accept as true my perceptual beliefs, my insights, my recollections, my inferences about the immediate state of affairs, so long as my mind is at ease about them. As regards spiritual leadings, this test is widely practiced among Quakers. Do not accept any leading, do not act on it, until your mind has weighed it well and is at ease with it. "Wear thy sword as long as thou canst," said Fox to the noble gentleman, William Penn. But this test alone seems more of a negative warning, when doubts occur, than a positive justification. It alone can't lead me to a divinity within.

2. *Reputable authority.* Depending on the context, the authority may be a newspaper, a newscaster, a teacher, a reference book, a parent, a wise friend, a political leader, a doctor, a leading scientist, a learned treatise—or holy writings and preachings. What makes a guide into a reputable authority? His background, his position in society, his plausibility, the fruits of his former activity, the tradition he speaks for, all may enter in. On spiritual matters, Locke, Fox, Rufus Jones and many others suggest that the most reputable authority for

testing our own insights is the Bible. Even if one doubts the Bible's divine inspiration, one may respect the spiritual authority of many who speak in it. They and others like them help form what Rufus Jones called the "illumination of History." But reliance on authority is just what I now was seeking to avoid.

3. *General consensus.* A large class of socially objective beliefs may be tested by the general consensus about them. Friends give weight to the consensus of members, not only on business matters but on social concerns. Beyond that, it used to be argued that God must exist because belief in God was virtually universal among humans. More recently it is claimed that God is dead because belief in God has diminished. Both of these arguments seem weak when applied to God. God's existence, whether within me or beyond me, depends not on social consensus but on the nature of reality.

4. *Correspondence with evidence.* This test is the one exalted by scientists (and rightly), especially when strict predictions can be derived from the belief and subjected to public verification or falsification. Less formally, the test is used also by detectives, reporters, lawyers and even housewives in testing a new product. Those who experience God directly in the form of inner visions or commands often cite their experience as experimental evidence. Unfortunately, however, this evidence is private rather than public, and it is hard to develop strict predictions from it.

5. *Coherence.* This means that the belief fits coherently with the whole body of our knowledge, or with relevant specialized knowledge. We often use this coherence test, sometimes casually, sometimes profoundly. And here if anywhere, I decided, I must find the way for testing whether the light within me is divine. The right path, I concluded, was to pose two questions: Given what we know about the human brain and what we know about operations of the inner light in its

various perspectives, is it plausible that all these latter operations are reducible to organic brain functioning? If not, is it plausible that the capacity for these operations is an aspect of God functioning in us?

These questions led me into extensive explorations, which carried me to some positive conclusions. And those conclusions have changed fundamentally my feeling about life. I shall now give the bare bones of the steps leading to these inferences, omitting much evidence.

BRAIN AND MIND

As to the brain and its functioning: recent decades have brought a massive quantity of brain research. Various specialized areas have been located among the brain's ten to twelve billion nerve cells. Yet no one has ever located an area where our enduring individual memories are stored. As the neurophysiologist Ralph W. Gerard reported, "Large sections of nearly any part of the brain can be destroyed without loss of particular memories or, indeed, without disturbance of the memory function."

Clearly the brain is our body's central control center. It receives and processes information. It monitors bodily functioning. It issues orders to the rest of the body. But does our brain do the *whole* job of our mind? There's good reason, I concluded, for supposing that a higher functional level than the brain is at work, at least in some of our achievements. One should note the great variability of human brains, the variations also in our life experiences, the constant remaking of the nerve cells' molecules, and the lack of any brain storage place for long-term individual memories. Let's pose these facts against some aspects of the four perspectives we discussed earlier.

First, certain abstract ideas are uniform or nearly uniform

among human beings able to attain to a certain level of thought. Thus people have been *seeing* various mathematical axioms and theorems in a similar way ever since Euclid. We today *see* logical principles, such as the principle of contradiction, like the Greeks. We feel a binding power from the ancient Golden Rule and the other moral principles cited by St. Augustine. The widespread uniformity of appeal exerted by these ideas can scarcely be explained in full as reactions in our so-different brains. Nor does it seem conceivable that a pattern for these ideas could be carried by the genetic code that exists in each of our trillions of body cells. Thus a new level of functioning must be introduced.

Second, some human minds seem to have extraordinary vision as regards the operations of nature. The scientific insights of such minds have moved the race remarkably far toward the truth about how the universe works. Consider the breakthroughs, not merely of technology but of theory, that lie behind splitting the atom or throwing a robot to Mars. As Einstein remarked, the real mystery of the universe is its comprehensibility. How is it possible that some of our minds can get so well attuned, not to the objects we handle every day, but to entities we can *never* handle—the immensely large and invisibly small—that we're able to formulate workable laws about how they function? Surely more than an evolution of brain cells is required to explain such cognitive leaps toward truth.

This quality of mind seems divinatory. That word comes from a remarkable scientist-philosopher, Charles Sanders Peirce. Here in part is what he said about it:

> Modern science has been builded after the model of Galileo, who founded it, on *il lume naturale*. That truly inspired prophet had said that, of two hypotheses, the *simpler* is to be preferred; but I was formerly one of those who, in our dull self-conceit fancying ourselves more sly than he, twisted the maxim to mean the *logically* simpler one, the one which adds the least to what has

> been observed. . . . It was not until long experience forced me to realize that subsequent discoveries were every time showing I had been wrong, while those who understood the maxim as Galileo had done, early unlocked the secret, that the scales fell from my eyes and my mind awoke to the broad and flaming daylight that it is the simpler hypothesis in the sense of the more facile and natural, the one that instinct suggests, that must be preferred; for the reason that, unless man have a natural bent in accordance with nature's, he has no chance of understanding nature at all. . . . it follows that man has, in some degree, a divinatory power, primary or derived. . . . *(Charles S. Peirce: Selected Writings,* ed. P. P. Wiener, pp. 372-3)

Peirce cited no examples, but one might adduce as divinatory leaps the heliocentric hypothesis of Copernicus and Galileo, the special relativity theory of Einstein, and the double helix model for the structure of DNA molecules put forward by Crick and Watson. This power to leap toward truth, not by building on past habits of thought but by overthrowing them, can scarcely be reduced to the movements of brain cells.

HUMAN INNERNESS

Third, my experience of innerness, the most fundamental experience of human beings, corresponds to nothing observable or describable in the physical realm, including the mini-realm of the brain cells. My innerness includes a variety of states. For example, I'm usually aware of a flow of events. In William James's words, the content of one's mind "is in a constant flux, events dawning into its forward end as fast as they fade out of its rearward end, and each of them changing its time-coefficient from 'not yet' or 'not quite yet' to 'just gone' or 'gone,' as it passes by." This awareness of flow, James noted in his *Principles of Psychology,* is quite different from a mere succession of physical events. "Even though we *were* to conceive the outer (physical) successions as forces stamping their image on the brain, and the brain's successions as forces stamping their image on the mind, still, between the mind's own changes *being* successive, and *knowing their own succession,* lies as broad a chasm as between the object and subject of any case of cognition in the world.''

My innerness can involve, too, a casting back in temporality or existential time to a sequence of past experiences that I can hold all-together-right-now (for example, events of the past three Sundays at meeting for worship), and these past events are ranged in order in a kind of inward temporal field. But my brain cells provide me with no such inward field and no imagery-clustered sequence of memories. Likewise I can project ahead into the not-yet-here my future plans and fears and dreams, in imagery that never before has appeared this way. My brain cells offer me no such futural field, stretching onward in temporality toward my death. Nor do they offer the kind of inner field used in creation by Nietzsche or Henry Moore.

Missing, too, from the brain is the subjective ''I'', the innermost self that I am, not my body, not my social self, not my experiences, but the ''I'' that wills my body to move, the ''I'' that acts and responds in the social world, the ''I'' that undergoes the experiences of living. This inmost self is what one means by 'I' when one says, ''I decided not to take the job'' or ''I hate spiders'' or ''I loved her for three years but I couldn't care less about her now.'' This is the ''I'' that can now remember the day of my college graduation, the day I married, the day each of my daughters was born, recalling those events not as neural traces but as sets of dim but evocative snapshots ranged in order of time. This ''I'' is always a subject (of sentences, of thought, of be-ing), never an object, never recorded in machine or device. This ''I'' is the subject of I-Thou loving. It is what *I am,* in essence. The brain cells have no place for it at all.

Here I had found three important kinds of human experience—uniform abstract ideas, a divinatory power of insight on nature, and personal innerness—that do not reduce plausibly to brain functioning alone. These kinds of experience are closely linked with that capacity called the inner light. Therefore I concluded that the inner light's operations are not fully reducible to brain functioning, even though the brain is obviously needed for the inner light to operate as we find it doing.

AN ASPECT OF GOD?

I turned then to the question of whether the inner light is, not metaphorically but literally, an aspect of God in us. To answer this I had to know what is God, if there *is* God. This task weighed on me more heavily than any other. How could I possibly answer such a question? Philosophers, theologians and ordinary people have disputed it for centuries. It seemed obvious, too, that whatever God is, *if* God is, must be far beyond human understanding. But to give up on the question would already be answering it "no." I tried to summon courage. Whatever I decided about it, I should probably look foolish to many. But did that matter? I needed an answer to satisfy myself, not to sound wise and worldly.

I decided to put aside temporarily the word 'God.' It has too many different meanings, too many overtones and undertones. I would deal instead with Ultimate Explanation, meaning by this the minimum nature of God.

I began with this proposition: Everything has some explanation. That is, nothing happens without some reason for it. Some physical cause or causes, or at least some other event or events, can explain, within the existing context, why what happened did happen. Of course we often don't know the true explanation. It may be very complex. We may never be able to unravel it. Our approach to truth—as I suggested in listing the various tests for truth—may always remain unsure and never rightly certain. Nonetheless, I thought, everything that happens does have *some* explanation. And by everything I meant not only physical things but also mental events and not only what's happening right now but what did happen and what may happen.

This principle that everything has an explanation is not provable by referring it to some more fundamental principle. It is itself a basic postulate for understanding the world. It's known as the principle of sufficient reason. The only way to check it out is to pick any object or any event whatever and ask yourself: Did this come to be without any reason at all, or does its existence have some explanation? You will probably agree that an explanation is required.

Now the scientific explanation offered for many events is a formula based on the statistical probability of event B following event A in context C. What this truly means is that we know only a part of the explanation for event B. The rest of the explanation may lie in unknown events or it may lie within the context, which may have some power of autonomous action. In some cases, as with quantum phenomena, we shall never know more than statistical laws. But even there I would hold, with Einstein, that the world in *reality* is not founded on the roll of dice. Even a quantum event has some explanation, though our instruments cannot reach it.

What happens when we try to push the "why" of an object or event back and back? Eventually we come to the laws of nature as science has formulated them. Necessary ingredients in deriving these laws are the principles of logic/mathematics. Also required are the "fields" of nature, namely (1) space or spacetime and (2) temporality or inward existential time. Lastly, in addition to laws of nature, principles of logic/mathematics and the two "fields," the universe also holds a vast creative evolving fund of energy. These seem to be the foundations that we reach as we strive to explain all that happens.

ULTIMATE EXPLANATION

Are these, then, the Ultimate Explanation, the foundation for the universe itself and all that is, was, and may come to be? No, not yet. For the laws of nature as we now formulate them are clearly not the complete and ultimate Laws of Nature that actually rule. The principles of logic/mathematics as we now know them, universal though they seem, and fanned out now into a variety of systems, are not necessarily the Formal Structure in full reality. As for the "fields," space or spacetime is only our view of Immensity; temporality or inward time is only our experience of the Eternal Now. Nature's creative evolving energy as we grasp it is no more than a pinch of Creativity itself. The Ultimate Explanation, then, is not what we have come to know but what lies behind what we now know: Laws of Nature, Formal Structure, Immensity, External Now, Creativity. This is not an imaginary God. It is God creating and sustaining the universe through each moment of its existence. And this Ultimate Explanation, in all of the above five aspects creates and sustains not only the universe but every component of the universe, including you and me. It's the existential ground of us all.

Thus God as Ultimate Explanation, functioning always and everywhere, functions also in each of us. And since the capacity we call the inner light does not reduce to brain functioning, and since we know of no other plausible source for it, it seems most likely that it is a direct case of God-functioning in us, imparting to us some slight measure of Godness.

But I found that this answer did not wholly satisfy. It seemed to me the universe holds more unity at its core than suggested by five separate aspects of Ultimate Explanation. Are these aspects not internally related? I felt pulled to go a bit beyond the evidence. I began to think the Laws of Nature, Formal

Structure, Immensity, Eternal Now, and Creativity are internally related by being known. A Divine Mind knows and thus unites them. By analogy our own limited minds know explanations and thus can begin to relate and unite them. And it's *this* quality of God, I thought, it's God as Ultimate Knower, that really touches us with the inner light, enabling us creatively to seek and reach some meanings, some explanations.

God as Ultimate Explanation and Knower is a minimum belief. Much else could be added. But a house needs first of all a firm foundation. And this belief is not an un-Christian view. I recalled the opening words of the Gospel of John: "In the beginning was the Word, and the Word was with God, and the Word was God." A peculiar assertion if you take it literally. But for St. John, in Greek, 'word' was *Logos*. And *Logos* meant not only 'word' but also other things including 'explanation.' In the beginning, then, was the ultimate explanation, and it was with God, and it was God: God knew it.

Gradually this belief took hold in me. I found myself surprisingly sustained. The inner light truly *is* a seed of God in me. The short deep emptiness that had seemed so trivial in my earlier experience with the light now took on a sweet warmth. At odd moments during the day I drift into it. It's always momentary. And it's always there, always sustaining when I touch it. I don't need a long straining effort to reach and grasp this sweet source. A moment's dropping down is enough. It's always present; I need not worry.

I began to lose my existential anxiety. I discovered since arriving at this belief, that I had come into existential delight. At times I still do fret, I get angry, I feel frustrations. But undergirding it all is a delight in living. Within me dwells an inner self that no storm can injure, no accident can maim, no malice can destroy. This inner self now feels free as never before, free from doubt and dread, free to move toward others, to love maturely, to seek truth and beauty, to weigh rightness in a new balance. And still I have far to go.

I end with three verses from Jan Luykens, a Dutch poet of the seventeenth century, in a translation by Frank Warnke:

> I thought that Godhead made its home afar,
> Enthroned beyond the moon and every star,
> And often lifted up my eyes
> Thither with deep and heartfelt sighs;
>
> But when it pleased thee to illuminate me,
> I saw no heavenly light descend to greet me;
> But at my spirit's deepest root
> All was lovely, all was sweet.
>
> For thou cam'st from the depths and outwards spread,
> And like a well my thirsty heart was fed;
> So was it, God, that thee I found
> To be the ground beneath my ground.

READING LIST

This list includes sources for the major quotations in the pamphlet, followed by suggestions for readers wishing to pursue some topics further.

St. Augustine. *Confessions,* tr. John K. Ryan. (Garden City, N.Y. Doubleday Image Books, 1960).

Berenson, Bernard. *Sketch for a Self-Portrait.* (Bloomington, Ind.: Indiana University Press, 1949). See p. 20.

Blackburn, E. A. ed. *A Treasury of the Kingdom.* (New York: Oxford University Press, 1954). For Blake quotation, p. 132.

Journal of George Fox, ed. by John L. Nickalls. (London: Religious Society of Friends, 1975).

Gerard, Ralph W. "What Is Memory?" In *Scientific American,* vol. 189 (1953), pp. 118-26.

Ghiselin, Brewster, ed. *The Creative Process.* (New York: New American Library, 1955). For Nietzsche, Picasso and Moore quotations.

Hocking, W. E. *The Meaning of Immortality in Human Experience.* (Westport, Conn.: Greenwood Publishers, 1973). See p. 232.

James, William. *The Principles of Psychology.* 2 vols. (New York: Dover Publications, 1950). See vol. 1, pp. 628-30.

Jones, Rufus M. *Quakerism: A Spiritual Movement.* (Philadelphia: Philadelphia Yearly Meeting of Friends, 1963).

________. *Studies in Spiritual Religion.* (New York: Russell & Russell, 1970).

Locke, John. *An Essay Concerning Human Understanding.* 2 vols. (New York: Dover Publications, 1959).

Charles S. Peirce: Selected Writings, ed. P. P. Wiener. (New York: Dover Publications, 1966).

Warnke, Frank J., ed. and tr. *European Metaphysical Poetry.* (New Haven: Yale University Press, 1974).

Whitehead, A. N. *Adventures of Ideas.* (New York: The Free Press, 1967). See p. 296.

On the philosophy and history of the inward light, I know of no fully adequate work. Apart from Rufus Jones' classic volumes, a fine account of a dozen great mystic visionaries will be found in Sheldon Cheney, *Men Who Have Walked with God* (New York: Knopf, 1968). Many rich insights on the light are contained in two books by Howard H. Brinton, *Friends for 300 Years* (Pendle Hill Publications, 1965) and *The Religious Philosophy of Quakerism* (Pendle Hill Publications, 1973). For a brief overview, see articles in *The New Catholic Encyclopedia* on "Light: Metaphysics of Light" and "Illumination."

On the non-identity of mind and brain, two books by noted brain scientists are of special interest: J. C. Eccles, *Facing Reality* (New York: Springer-Verlag, 1970) and Wilder Penfield, *The Mystery of the Mind* (Princeton: Princeton University Press, 1975). See also my article on memory in the *Journal of Phenomenological Psychology,* vol. 7, no. 1, Fall, 1976.

On meeting for worship and how to approach it, I have found several pamphlets enlightening. Four are by Douglas V. Steere, *On Being Present Where You Are* (Pendle Hill Pamphlet 151), *On Speaking Out of the Silence* (Pendle Hill Pamphlet 182), *Where Words Come From* (London: Friends Home Service Committee, 1968), and a small leaflet, *A Quaker Meeting for Worship* (Friends General Conference). Other publications on the subject are Howard E. Collier's *The Quaker Meeting* (Pendle Hill Pamphlet 26), and a leaflet by Thomas R. Kelly, *The Gathered Meeting* (Philadelphia: Friends Tract Association, 1957).